HOW TO START A COFFEE TRUCK BUSINESS

Essential Strategies For Success In The Mobile Coffee Industry

Sophia Williams

Copyright Page

How to start a coffee truck business

Author: *Sophia Williams*

Copyright © [2024] by [Sophia Williams]

All rights reserved. No part of this book may be reproduced, distributed, or transmitted in any form or by any means, including photocopying, recording, or other electronic or mechanical methods, without the prior written permission of the publisher, except in the case of brief quotations embodied in critical reviews and certain other non-commercial uses permitted by copyright law.

Printed in the United States of America

Thank you for respecting the hard work of this author.

Contents

Copyright Page 2

Chapter 1: Introduction to the Coffee Truck Business 7

   1.1 The Rise of Mobile Coffee Culture 7

   1.2 Why Start a Coffee Truck? 7

   1.3 Defining Your Vision 8

Chapter 2: Planning and Setting Up Your Coffee Truck 11

   1. Business Planning and Structure 11

Writing a Comprehensive Business Plan comes first in your business Structure and a well-crafted business plan is the backbone of any successful business, and your coffee truck is no exception. This document will serve as your roadmap, guiding your decisions and helping you stay on track as you build and grow your business. Here's a breakdown of what to include: 11

   2. Choosing the Right Business Structure 13

3. Understanding Legal Requirements and Permits 14

Budgeting and Financing Your Coffee Truck 15

    Estimating Start-Up Costs 15

    Exploring Funding Options 17

    Managing Operational Expenses 18

    Selecting and Outfitting Your Truck 19

    Essential Equipment and Layout Considerations 21

    Customization and Branding Your Truck's Exterior 23

Chapter 3: Sourcing and Managing Your Coffee and Supplies ... 25

    Understanding Coffee Beans and Their Origins 25

    Sourcing High-Quality Coffee Beans 26

    Selecting a Coffee Supplier 27

        Sourcing Other Key Ingredients and Supplies 28

    Managing Inventory and Supply Chain 31

    Reducing Waste and Maximizing Efficiency 32

Chapter 6 51

Operational Efficiency and Scaling Your Coffee Truck Business. 51

Streamlining Daily Operations 51

Enhancing Customer Experience 52

Scaling Your Coffee Truck Business 53

Managing Challenges During Growth 54

CONCLUSION 57

Ensuring Consistency and Quality Control: Developing Standard Operating Procedures (SOPs 33

Customer Feedback and Continuous Improvement 34

Chapter 4 35

Navigating Legal Requirements and Health Regulations. 35

Understanding the Legal Structure of Your Business 35

Securing the Necessary Permits and Licenses 36

Health and Safety Regulations 38

Understanding Zoning Laws and Parking Restrictions 40

Liability Insurance and Risk Management 41

Chapter 5 45

Marketing and Building a Loyal Customer Base 45

Crafting a Unique Brand Identity 45

Leveraging Digital Marketing Channels 46

Creating Memorable Customer Experiences 47

Measuring and Analyzing Marketing Success 49

Chapter 1: Introduction to the Coffee Truck Business

1.1 The Rise of Mobile Coffee Culture

The world of coffee has evolved dramatically over the past few decades, transforming from a simple morning ritual into a vibrant, ever-expanding culture. Among the most exciting developments in this space is the rise of mobile coffee trucks. These unique businesses have capitalized on the increasing demand for specialty coffee, offering consumers high-quality beverages on the go. With the flexibility to pop up at various locations—from bustling city centers to local farmers' markets—coffee trucks provide a fresh, convenient, and personalized coffee experience.

Unlike traditional brick-and-mortar coffee shops, mobile coffee trucks can adapt to changing consumer trends, meet customers where they are, and offer a more intimate and customizable experience. Whether parked at a music festival, a corporate event, or simply a street corner with heavy foot traffic, these trucks bring the art of coffee-making directly to the consumer, blending convenience with quality in a way that is both novel and appealing.

1.2 Why Start a Coffee Truck?

Starting a coffee truck business presents a unique opportunity for aspiring entrepreneurs to dive into the booming coffee industry without the hefty upfront costs associated with opening a traditional café. With lower overhead, greater flexibility, and the ability to move where demand is highest, coffee trucks offer several advantages that are particularly attractive to those new to the food and beverage industry.

However, like any business, running a coffee truck comes with its own set of challenges. Limited space, weather dependency, and the need to constantly attract new customers are just a few of the obstacles that operators must navigate. But with careful planning, a strong work ethic, and a passion for coffee, these challenges can be managed and even turned into opportunities for growth.

This chapter will guide you through the initial steps of launching your coffee truck, helping you weigh the pros and cons and providing you with the knowledge needed to start on the right foot.

1.3 Defining Your Vision

Before you can brew your first cup or serve your first customer, it's essential to have a clear vision for your coffee truck business. This vision will guide every decision you make, from the type of coffee you serve to the way you interact with your customers. A well-defined vision not only helps you stay focused and motivated but also sets you apart in a competitive market.

Start by setting specific goals for your coffee truck. Are you looking to create a boutique coffee experience with artisanal drinks? Do you want to offer quick, affordable coffee options to busy commuters? Or perhaps you aim to bring a slice of your local culture to the wider community through your mobile café? Whatever your goals, they should be reflected in every aspect of your business, from your branding to your customer service.

Identifying your unique selling proposition (USP) is another critical step. This is what makes your coffee truck stand out from the competition. Whether it's a signature drink, a focus on sustainability, or a particular style of customer service, your USP will be the cornerstone of your brand.

Finally, understanding your target market is crucial. Who are your customers, and what do they value? Are they coffee aficionados looking for the perfect brew, or are they casual drinkers in search of a convenient caffeine fix? By defining your target audience, you can tailor your offerings and marketing strategies to meet their needs, ensuring that your coffee truck resonates with the right people from day one.

In this book, we'll explore how to craft a vision that not only reflects your passion but also aligns with market demands, setting you up for success as you embark on your coffee truck journey.

"Success is brewing with every cup you serve—believe in your blend and let your passion be the fuel that drives your journey."

2. Choosing the Right Business Structure

Selecting the appropriate legal structure for your coffee truck business is a critical decision that will impact your taxes, liability, and day-to-day operations. Here's a closer look at the most common options:

Sole Proprietorship: This is the simplest business structure, where you, as the owner, are the sole decision-maker. It's easy to set up and offers complete control, but it also means you are personally liable for any debts or legal actions against the business.

Partnership: If you plan to start the business with one or more partners, a partnership structure might be suitable. There are two main types: general partnerships (where all partners share liability and management responsibilities) and limited partnerships (where some partners have limited liability and involvement). Be sure to draft a partnership agreement to outline each partner's role and share of profits.

Limited Liability Company (LLC): An LLC combines the liability protection of a corporation with the tax benefits and operational flexibility of a partnership. This structure is popular among small business owners because it protects your personal assets while allowing you to avoid double taxation.

Corporation: A corporation is a more complex structure that involves more regulatory requirements and tax obligations. It's typically not necessary for a small coffee truck business but could be considered if you plan to scale significantly or bring in multiple investors.

3. Understanding Legal Requirements and Permits

Running a coffee truck involves navigating a web of legal requirements and permits. These regulations vary by location, so it's essential to research the specific rules in your area. Here are some key considerations:

- **Business License:** Most municipalities require a general business license to operate. This permits you to legally conduct business within the jurisdiction.

- **Food Truck Permit:** A specific permit for operating a mobile food business is usually required. This permit often involves a health inspection to ensure your truck meets sanitation and safety standards.

- **Health Department Permit:** As a food service provider, you'll need to comply with local health department regulations. This includes regular inspections and adherence to food safety practices.

- **Zoning Permits:** Since your truck will operate in various locations, you must understand local zoning laws. Some areas may have restrictions on where food trucks can park and operate.

- **Fire Safety Permit:** Because your coffee truck will likely use equipment that involves heat, such as espresso machines and coffee brewers, a fire safety permit may be required. Ensure that your truck is equipped with the necessary fire safety equipment, such as fire extinguishers.

- **Signage Permits:** If you plan to display signs or banners outside your truck, you may need a signage permit, depending on local regulations.

Budgeting and Financing Your Coffee Truck

Estimating Start-Up Costs

Before you start serving your first cup of coffee, you need to have a clear understanding of the costs involved in setting up your coffee truck. These can vary widely depending on factors like your location, the type of truck you choose, and the quality of the equipment you purchase. Here's a detailed breakdown of the main expenses:

1. **Vehicle Purchase or Lease:** The cost of the truck itself is likely to be your largest upfront expense. You can either buy a new or used truck, or lease one, depending on your budget and long-term plans. Expect to spend anywhere from $10,000 to $100,000 depending on the truck's condition, size, and customization needs.

2. **Equipment:** Your coffee truck will require specialized equipment, including espresso machines, grinders, coffee brewers, refrigerators, sinks, and water tanks. High-quality equipment can be costly, but it's crucial for maintaining consistency and quality in your product. Budget at least $15,000 to $30,000 for equipment.

3. **Truck Customization:** Customizing your truck to meet health and safety standards, as well as creating an efficient and aesthetically pleasing layout, can add to your costs. This includes plumbing, electrical work, installing countertops, storage units, and more. Customization costs can range from $10,000 to $50,000.

4. **Licenses and Permits:** As discussed earlier, you'll need to budget for various licenses and permits. These costs can range from a few hundred to several thousand dollars depending on your location.

5. **Initial Inventory:** Stocking up on high-quality coffee beans, milk, syrups, cups, lids, and other supplies will require an initial investment. Plan to spend $1,000 to $5,000 on your first batch of inventory.

6. **Branding and Marketing:** Developing your brand identity, including designing a logo, creating signage, and launching a website or social media presence, will also incur costs. Set aside $2,000 to $5,000 for these initial marketing expenses.

7. **Insurance:** Protecting your business with the right insurance coverage is essential. This includes general liability, vehicle, and possibly workers' compensation insurance if you have employees. Insurance costs can range from $1,000 to $5,000 annually.

8. **Miscellaneous Costs:** Don't forget to budget for other expenses such as uniforms, point-of-sale systems, and initial working capital to cover operating costs until your business becomes profitable.

Exploring Funding Options

Once you have a clear understanding of your startup costs, the next step is to secure the necessary funding. There are several ways to finance your coffee truck business, A few of them have been analyzed below.

Personal Savings: If you have savings, using them to fund your business can be a good option, as it avoids the need to take on debt. However, be cautious about depleting your personal savings entirely.

Small Business Loans: Banks and credit unions often offer small business loans to entrepreneurs. To qualify, you'll need a solid business plan, a good credit score, and possibly collateral. Consider applying for loans specifically designed for small businesses, such as those backed by the Small Business Administration (SBA) in the U.S.

Microloans: Microloans are smaller loans, typically under $50,000, offered by non-profit organizations and community lenders. These loans are often easier to obtain than traditional bank loans and are ideal for startups with lower capital needs.

Equipment Financing: Some lenders offer loans or leases specifically for purchasing equipment. This allows you to spread the cost of your coffee truck's equipment over time rather than paying for it all upfront.

Crowdfunding: Platforms like Kickstarter, Indiegogo, or GoFundMe allow you to raise funds from the public. In exchange for financial contributions, you can offer rewards such as free coffee, branded merchandise, or special discounts.

Investors: If you're open to sharing ownership of your business, you might consider bringing on investors. This could be family members, friends, or professional investors who provide capital in exchange for equity in your company.

Grants: Depending on your location, you might be eligible for grants aimed at supporting small businesses or specific types of entrepreneurs, such as women, minorities, or veterans. Research local and national grant opportunities that align with your business.

Managing Operational Expenses

Once your coffee truck is up and running, it's important to keep a close eye on your operational expenses to ensure long-term profitability. Some key areas to manage are: Inventory Management, Labor Costs, Fuel and Maintenance, Utilities, Marketing and Advertising, Insurance Premiums and Miscellaneous Expenses e.t.c.

- **Inventory Management:** Regularly monitor your inventory to avoid overstocking or running out of supplies. Implement an inventory management system to track usage and automate reordering.

- **Labor Costs:** If you plan to hire employees, labor will be one of your significant ongoing expenses. Manage labor costs by optimizing your schedule, cross-training staff to perform multiple roles, and minimizing overtime.

- **Fuel and Maintenance:** As a mobile business, fuel and vehicle maintenance are regular costs you'll need to budget for. Perform routine maintenance to prevent costly repairs and ensure your truck is always operational.

- **Utilities:** Although your utility costs will be lower than a brick-and-mortar café, you'll still need to budget for electricity (for equipment), water, and potentially a commissary kitchen rental if required by local regulations.

- **Marketing and Advertising:** Ongoing marketing efforts are crucial to attract and retain customers. Allocate a portion of your budget for digital marketing, promotions, and participation in local events.

- **Insurance Premiums:** Ensure your insurance coverage is up to date and budget for annual premium payments.

- **Miscellaneous Expenses:** Be prepared for unexpected costs, such as repairs, permit renewals, and seasonal fluctuations in business.

Selecting and Outfitting Your Truck

Selecting the right vehicle is one of the most critical decisions you'll make when setting up your coffee truck. The vehicle you choose will impact your operational efficiency, customer experience, and overall brand image. Here's what to consider when choosing or selecting your business truck.

Size and Layout: The size of your truck will depend on your menu, equipment needs, and staffing requirements. Ensure the truck has enough space for your coffee equipment, supplies, and staff to work comfortably. A well-thought-out layout is crucial for efficient workflow and quick service.

New vs. Used: Deciding whether to buy a new or used truck will depend on your budget and long-term goals. A new truck can be customized to your exact specifications and may come with warranties, but it's more expensive. A used truck is more affordable but may require more maintenance and retrofitting to meet your needs.

Type of Truck: You'll need to choose between different types of vehicles, such as step vans, food trucks, or trailers. Step vans are popular for coffee trucks due to their spacious interiors and durability. Trailers can be a cost-effective option, but they require a tow vehicle.

Fuel Type: Consider whether you want a gas-powered, diesel, or electric vehicle. Diesel trucks are known for their durability and fuel efficiency, but they may have higher maintenance costs. Electric trucks are more environmentally friendly and can reduce fuel costs but may have limited range and higher upfront costs.

Customization Potential: Ensure the truck you choose can be customized to accommodate all your equipment and branding needs. Some trucks come partially outfitted for food service, which can reduce customization costs.

Essential Equipment and Layout Considerations

Outfitting your truck with the right equipment is crucial for delivering high-quality coffee and ensuring smooth operations. Here's a list of few necessary equipments:

- **Espresso Machine:** The espresso machine is the heart of your coffee truck. Choose a commercial-grade machine that can handle high volumes and deliver consistent quality. Consider whether you want a traditional machine (which requires more skill) or an automatic or semi-automatic machine (which is easier to use but offers less control).

- **Coffee Grinder:** A high-quality grinder is essential for producing fresh, evenly ground coffee. Opt for a burr grinder, which offers more consistent grinds than a blade grinder. You may need multiple grinders if you plan to offer different types of coffee, such as espresso and drip coffee.

- **Coffee Brewer:** In addition to espresso, you may want to offer brewed coffee. A commercial coffee brewer allows you to serve large quantities quickly. Consider whether you want a drip brewer, pour-over station, or other brewing methods like French press or cold brew.

- **Refrigeration:** You'll need refrigeration to store milk, cream, and other perishables. Depending on your menu, you may also need freezers for items like ice cream or frozen drinks. Make sure your refrigeration units are energy-efficient and compact enough to fit in your truck.

- **Water Supply and Filtration:** A reliable water supply is essential for making coffee and maintaining cleanliness. Install a high-quality water filtration system to ensure the best-tasting coffee and to protect your equipment from mineral buildup. Your truck will also need a water tank and waste water tank that meet local health regulations.

- **Sinks and Handwashing Stations:** Health codes typically require a minimum number of sinks for washing hands, utensils, and equipment. Make sure your truck is equipped with the necessary sinks and that they are easily accessible.

- **Storage Solutions:** Efficient storage is crucial in a small space. Invest in shelving, cabinets, and storage bins to keep your supplies organized and within easy reach. Consider vertical storage solutions to maximize space.

- **POS System:** A reliable point-of-sale (POS) system is essential for processing payments, tracking sales, and managing inventory. Choose a mobile-friendly system that integrates with your accounting software and offers features like customer loyalty programs and sales analytics.

- **Ventilation and Exhaust:** Proper ventilation is essential for maintaining a comfortable working environment and complying with health regulations. Ensure your truck has a commercial-grade hood and exhaust system to remove steam, heat, and odors.

- **Lighting:** Good lighting is important for both safety and aesthetics. Install adequate task lighting in the work area and ambient lighting for customer-facing areas.

- **Safety Equipment:** Your truck should be equipped with fire extinguishers, first aid kits, and non-slip flooring to ensure the safety of your staff and customers.

Customization and Branding Your Truck's Exterior

Your coffee truck's exterior is the first thing customers will see, so it's important to make a strong visual impression. The design of your truck should reflect your brand's personality and appeal to your target audience. Consider working with a professional designer to create a cohesive look that includes your logo, color scheme, and graphics. The design should be eye-catching, memorable, and consistent with your brand identity.

Clear, visible signage is essential for attracting customers and communicating your offerings. Invest in high-quality, weather-resistant signs that display your logo, menu, and any specials or promotions. Consider digital menu boards that can be easily updated or chalkboards for a more rustic, personalized touch.

A full vehicle wrap can transform your truck into a mobile billboard, showcasing your brand wherever you go. Wraps are a popular option because they're durable, customizable, and can cover the entire truck. Decals are a more affordable alternative and can be used to highlight specific elements like your logo or social media handles. Exterior lighting is important for visibility, especially if you operate in the early morning or late evening. Consider installing LED lights around your service window and under awnings to create a welcoming ambiance. Decorative lighting can also enhance the aesthetic appeal of your truck.

The service window is where all the action happens, so it should be functional and inviting. Ensure that it's large enough for efficient service and consider adding an awning to protect customers from the elements. An awning can also serve as additional branding space.

If sustainability is part of your brand, consider eco-friendly customizations such as solar panels, biodegradable packaging, or a green roof. These features not only align with your brand values but can also attract environmentally-conscious customers.

Engage your customers by adding interactive elements to your truck's exterior. This could include a suggestion box, social media wall, or a small seating area with branded chairs and tables if space allows.

This chapter provides a comprehensive guide to the planning and setup phase of your coffee truck business. By carefully considering each aspect—from business planning and financing to vehicle selection and customization—you'll be well-prepared to launch a successful and sustainable coffee truck that stands out in the competitive mobile coffee market.

Chapter 3: Sourcing and Managing Your Coffee and Supplies

We'll now move into the crucial aspects of sourcing and managing the coffee and supplies that will be the backbone of your coffee truck business. Quality ingredients, reliable suppliers, and efficient inventory management are essential to ensuring that your coffee truck runs smoothly and consistently delivers top-notch beverages. This chapter will guide you through the entire process, from selecting the best coffee beans to managing your supply chain and inventory.

Understanding Coffee Beans and Their Origins

The Basics of Coffee Beans

Before you can serve the perfect cup of coffee, it's essential to understand the basics of coffee beans and how they impact the flavor of your beverages. Coffee beans are the seeds of the coffee cherry, and they come in various types, each with distinct characteristics. Here are the most common types:

- **Arabica vs. Robusta:** Arabica beans are the most popular, known for their smooth, complex flavors and lower caffeine content. They are generally considered higher quality and are often used in specialty coffee. Robusta beans, on the other hand, have a stronger, more bitter taste with higher caffeine content. They are often used in espresso blends and instant coffee.

- **Single-Origin vs. Blends:** Single-origin coffee comes from a specific region or farm, offering unique flavors that reflect the terroir of the area. Blends combine beans from multiple origins to create a balanced flavor profile.

Both options have their advantages, depending on the experience you want to offer your customers.

- **Processing Methods:** The way coffee beans are processed after harvesting affects their flavor. Common methods include washed (wet) processing, which produces a clean, bright flavor; natural (dry) processing, which enhances fruity and sweet notes; and honey processing, which offers a balance between the two.

- **Roast Levels:** Coffee beans can be roasted at various levels, from light to dark. Light roasts retain more of the bean's original flavor, highlighting acidity and fruitiness. Medium roasts offer a balance of flavor, body, and acidity, while dark roasts are bolder, with a more pronounced roasted flavor and lower acidity.

Sourcing High-Quality Coffee Beans

Finding the right coffee beans is critical to the success of your coffee truck. Your beans will determine the flavor, aroma, and overall quality of your coffee, so it's essential to choose wisely. Here are some strategies for sourcing high-quality beans:

Building Relationships with Coffee Roasters: Partnering with a reputable coffee roaster can be one of the best ways to ensure you're getting high-quality beans. Roasters often have strong connections with coffee growers and can offer expert advice on which beans to choose. Look for a roaster who shares your commitment to quality and sustainability.

Direct Trade vs. Fair Trade: If sustainability and ethical sourcing are important to your brand, consider the difference between direct trade and fair trade. Direct trade involves building direct relationships with coffee farmers, often leading to higher quality beans and better prices for growers. Fair trade, on the other hand, is a certification that ensures farmers receive fair wages and work in safe conditions.

Sampling and Cupping: Before committing to a particular bean or roaster, request samples and conduct a cupping session—a standardized method of tasting coffee to evaluate its flavor profile. This process allows you to compare different beans and choose the ones that best match your desired flavor profile.

Seasonality and Freshness: Coffee is a seasonal crop, so the availability of certain beans can fluctuate throughout the year. Stay informed about the harvest cycles of different coffee-growing regions to ensure you're sourcing the freshest beans. Consider rotating your offerings based on seasonal availability to keep your menu interesting and dynamic.

Organic and Specialty Coffees: Depending on your target market, you might want to offer organic or specialty-grade coffee. Organic coffee is grown without synthetic pesticides or fertilizers, appealing to health-conscious consumers. Specialty-grade coffee is scored 80 or above on a 100-point scale and is known for its exceptional quality.

Selecting a Coffee Supplier

Once you've determined the type of coffee beans you want to use, the next step is selecting a reliable supplier.

Supplier Reputation: Research potential suppliers and read reviews from other coffee businesses. A supplier's reputation in the industry is a good indicator of their reliability and the quality of their products.

Delivery and Lead Times: Consider the supplier's delivery schedule and lead times. You'll need a supplier who can consistently deliver fresh beans in a timely manner, ensuring that you never run out of stock.

Pricing and Terms: Compare pricing from different suppliers, but remember that cheaper isn't always better. Look for a balance between cost and quality. Also, review the supplier's payment terms and minimum order requirements to ensure they align with your cash flow and storage capacity.

Sustainability and Ethical Practices: If sustainability is part of your brand, choose a supplier who shares your values. Ask about their sourcing practices, environmental initiatives, and support for coffee-growing communities.

Support and Training: Some suppliers offer additional support, such as training on coffee brewing techniques or marketing assistance. These added services can be valuable, especially if you're new to the coffee industry.

Sourcing Other Key Ingredients and Supplies

Beyond coffee beans, other ingredients like milk, dairy alternatives, and syrups play a significant role in the flavor and texture of your beverages. Here's how to source the best:

1. **Milk:** If you're using dairy milk, choose high-quality, fresh milk from a reputable supplier. Consider offering different types of milk, such as whole, skim, and half-and-half, to cater to varying customer preferences. The quality of the milk can significantly affect the texture and taste of your lattes, cappuccinos, and other milk-based drinks.

2. **Dairy Alternatives:** With the growing demand for plant-based options, offering dairy alternatives like almond, soy, oat, or coconut milk is essential. Test different brands to find the ones that froth well and complement the flavor of your coffee. Be mindful of any potential allergens and clearly label your offerings.

3. **Syrups and Flavorings:** Syrups and flavorings allow you to create a variety of flavored coffee drinks, from vanilla lattes to caramel macchiatos. Source high-quality, natural syrups free from artificial additives. Consider offering seasonal flavors like pumpkin spice or peppermint to keep your menu fresh and exciting.

The presentation of your coffee is just as important as its flavor, making cups, lids, and packaging key components of your business. Choose sturdy, heat-resistant cups that maintain the temperature of your beverages without leaking or burning customers' hands. Consider offering a range of sizes to accommodate different drink preferences. Lids should fit securely and be easy to drink from. Consider eco-friendly options like compostable or recyclable cups and lids to appeal to environmentally-conscious customers.

Your cups and packaging are prime real estate for branding. Custom-printed cups with your logo and design can enhance brand recognition and create a professional appearance. You can also use this space to communicate your brand values, such as sustainability or community involvement. Don't overlook the smaller items like napkins, straws, and cup sleeves. These should be functional and match the quality of the rest of your packaging. Again, consider eco-friendly materials to minimize your environmental impact.

To keep your coffee truck running smoothly, you'll need a variety of additional supplies. Such as:

Cleaning Supplies: Maintaining a clean environment is essential for both hygiene and customer satisfaction. Stock up on cleaning supplies such as dish soap, sanitizing sprays, sponges, and microfiber cloths. Ensure that your staff follows a strict cleaning schedule to keep the truck spotless.

Maintenance Supplies: Regular maintenance of your coffee equipment is critical to avoid breakdowns and ensure consistent quality. Keep a supply of spare parts, lubricants, and cleaning kits specific to your espresso machine, grinder, and other equipment.

Utensils and Tools: You'll need a range of utensils and tools, including spoons, measuring scoops, tampers, milk frothing pitchers, and thermometers. Invest in high-quality, durable tools that will stand up to daily use.

Managing Inventory and Supply Chain

Effective inventory management is crucial to ensuring that you always have the necessary supplies on hand without overstocking. Here's how to manage your inventory efficiently:

Choosing an Inventory Management System: Invest in an inventory management system that tracks your supplies in real time, alerts you when stock is low, and generates reports on usage patterns. There are many software options available, from simple spreadsheet-based systems to more sophisticated, cloud-based solutions.

Setting Par Levels: Establish par levels (the minimum amount of stock you need to have on hand) for each item, based on your sales data and supplier lead times. This helps you reorder supplies before you run out.

Conducting Regular Inventory Audits: Perform regular inventory audits to compare your actual stock levels with your inventory records. This helps you identify discrepancies, prevent theft, and reduce waste.

FIFO (First-In, First-Out): Implement the FIFO method to ensure that older stock is used before new stock. This is particularly important for perishable items like coffee beans and dairy products, as it helps prevent spoilage.

A well-organized supply chain ensures that your coffee truck operates smoothly and efficiently. Build strong relationships with your suppliers to ensure reliable and timely deliveries. Communicate regularly and clearly about your needs, and address any issues promptly to avoid disruptions.

Decide whether to purchase supplies in bulk or use a just-in-time approach. Bulk purchasing can save money and reduce the frequency of orders, but it requires more storage space. Just-in-time purchasing minimizes storage needs and keeps your inventory fresh but may lead to stockouts if there are delays in delivery.

Be aware of your suppliers' lead times and plan your orders accordingly. If a particular item has a long lead time, order it well in advance to avoid running out. Consider the environmental impact of your supply chain. This might include choosing local suppliers to reduce transportation emissions, selecting products with minimal packaging, or working with suppliers who use sustainable practices.

Reducing Waste and Maximizing Efficiency

Reducing waste is not only environmentally responsible but also cost-effective. Here's how to minimize waste and maximize efficiency:

- **Portion Control:** Use portion control tools to ensure consistent serving sizes and reduce waste. This applies to both coffee grounds and additional ingredients like syrups and milk.

- **Recycling and Composting:** Implement a recycling and composting program to reduce waste. Many coffee-related items, such as used grounds, coffee filters, and even some cups, can be composted. Recycling bins for paper, plastics, and metals should be easily accessible to both staff and customers.

- **Repurposing and Upcycling:** Get creative with ways to repurpose waste. For example, used coffee grounds can be donated to local gardens as fertilizer or used to make coffee-based scrubs and soaps.

- **Energy and Water Efficiency:** Choose energy-efficient equipment and train your staff to minimize water and energy use. Simple actions like turning off equipment when not in use and fixing leaks promptly can lead to significant savings over time.

Ensuring Consistency and Quality Control: Developing Standard Operating Procedures (SOPs)

To ensure that every cup of coffee you serve meets your quality standards, it's essential to develop and implement Standard Operating Procedures (SOPs).

Recipe Standardization: Standardize all your coffee recipes, including the amount of coffee, water, milk, and flavorings used. This ensures that your beverages taste the same every time, regardless of who is making them.

Training and Documentation: Document your SOPs in a clear, easy-to-follow format and provide thorough training for your staff. This might include step-by-step instructions, videos, and hands-on practice sessions.

Quality Control Checks: Implement regular quality control checks to ensure that your SOPs are being followed. This could involve taste tests, equipment inspections, and reviewing customer feedback.

Customer Feedback and Continuous Improvement

Listening to your customers and making continuous improvements based on their feedback is key to maintaining high-quality service: Make it easy for customers to provide feedback, whether through comment cards, social media, or your website. Regularly review this feedback to identify areas for improvement.

If customers raise concerns about the quality of your coffee or service, address them quickly and professionally. Use these experiences as learning opportunities to prevent similar issues in the future. Ongoing training for your staff is essential to maintaining quality. Regularly update your training materials and provide refresher courses to ensure that everyone is up to date with the latest techniques and standards.

Chapter 4

Navigating Legal Requirements and Health Regulations.

Launching a coffee truck business involves more than just brewing great coffee; it also requires navigating a complex web of legal requirements and health regulations. This chapter will guide you through the essential legal steps and health considerations necessary to operate your coffee truck smoothly and compliantly. By understanding the legal landscape, securing the right permits, and adhering to health standards, you'll be able to avoid costly fines, ensure the safety of your customers, and build a reputable business.

Understanding the Legal Structure of Your Business

Before you can hit the road, it's crucial to establish the legal structure of your coffee truck business. This decision will affect your taxes, liability, and ability to raise capital, so it's important to choose the right structure from the outset. The most common legal structures for small businesses include sole proprietorship, partnership, limited liability company (LLC), and corporation.

1. **Sole Proprietorship:** As the simplest and most common form of business structure, a sole proprietorship involves a single individual owning and operating the business. It's easy to set up and offers complete control to the owner. However, the major drawback is that there's no legal distinction between the owner and the business, meaning you're personally liable for all debts and legal actions against the business.

2. **Partnership:** If you're starting your coffee truck with one or more partners, a partnership might be the right choice. Partnerships allow you to share the profits, losses, and management responsibilities with your partners. However, similar to a sole

proprietorship, partners are personally liable for business debts and obligations. To mitigate potential conflicts, it's essential to have a detailed partnership agreement outlining each partner's role, investment, and profit-sharing arrangement.

3. **Limited Liability Company (LLC):** An LLC combines the liability protection of a corporation with the tax benefits and flexibility of a partnership. As an LLC owner, you're not personally liable for the business's debts or legal issues. This structure is particularly popular among small business owners because it provides protection without the complexity and formalities of a corporation. Additionally, LLCs offer flexible tax options, allowing you to choose how the business's income is taxed.

4. **Corporation:** A corporation is a more complex business structure that is legally separate from its owners. This means that shareholders (owners) are not personally liable for the corporation's debts or legal issues. Corporations can raise capital by issuing stock, making them a good option if you plan to expand your business significantly. However, corporations are subject to more regulations, require more extensive record-keeping, and face double taxation (corporate income is taxed, and shareholders are also taxed on dividends).

5. Once you've chosen the legal structure, you'll need to register your business with the appropriate state and local authorities. This process typically involves filing the necessary paperwork, paying a registration fee, and obtaining a business license. The specific requirements vary by location, so it's essential to research the regulations in your area.

Securing the Necessary Permits and Licenses

Operating a coffee truck requires several permits and licenses to ensure you comply with local, state, and federal regulations. These permits vary depending on your location and the nature of your business, but some are universally required for mobile food businesses.

Business License: This is a general license required to operate any type of business legally within a particular jurisdiction. It allows you to conduct business activities in your city or county and must be obtained before you start operating your coffee truck. The application process usually involves providing details about your business, such as its name, address, and the nature of the services you'll provide. Be prepared to pay a fee, which varies depending on your location.

Health Department Permit: As a food service business, your coffee truck must meet specific health and safety standards. The health department permit ensures that your truck, equipment, and food handling practices comply with local health regulations. To obtain this permit, your truck will need to undergo a health inspection, during which an inspector will assess the cleanliness of your vehicle, the safety of your food storage and preparation areas, and the proper handling of ingredients. You may also need to attend a food safety course and pass an exam to demonstrate your knowledge of food handling and sanitation practices.

Mobile Food Vendor Permit: Many cities require a specific permit for mobile food vendors. This permit allows you to operate a food truck within designated areas and usually comes with a list of rules you must follow, such as where you can park, hours of operation, and waste disposal requirements. Some cities limit the number of food truck permits issued, so it's important to apply early and ensure you meet all the criteria.

Fire Department Permit: Coffee trucks, like other food trucks, often involve the use of equipment that poses a fire risk, such as propane tanks, generators, and cooking appliances. A fire department permit ensures that your truck is equipped with the necessary fire safety equipment, such as fire extinguishers and smoke detectors, and that your setup complies with local fire codes. The fire department may conduct an inspection to verify that your truck is safe for operation.

Commissary Agreement: In some areas, food trucks are required to have a commissary or commercial kitchen that they return to daily for food preparation, storage, and waste disposal. A commissary agreement is a contract with a licensed kitchen facility that you'll use for these purposes. This requirement is in place to ensure that food trucks have access to adequate facilities for maintaining cleanliness and food safety. The commissary agreement must be submitted as part of your permit application, and the facility may also be subject to inspection.

Signage and Advertising Permits: If you plan to use signs, banners, or other advertising materials on your truck, you may need a signage permit. This permit ensures that your advertising complies with local zoning laws and aesthetic guidelines. Some areas have strict regulations regarding the size, placement, and content of signage, so it's important to check with your local planning department before designing your truck's exterior.

Navigating the permit and licensing process can be complex and time-consuming, but it's a critical step in ensuring your coffee truck operates legally and smoothly. Keep in mind that regulations can change, so it's essential to stay informed and renew your permits and licenses as required.

Health and Safety Regulations

Health and safety are paramount in the food service industry, and as a coffee truck owner, it's your responsibility to ensure that your operations meet all required standards. Failure to comply with health and safety regulations can lead to fines, closures, and damage to your reputation. This section will cover the key health and safety regulations you need to follow.

Food Handling and Sanitation: Proper food handling practices are essential to prevent foodborne illnesses and ensure the safety of your customers. This includes maintaining clean and sanitized equipment, washing hands frequently, and using gloves when handling ready-to-eat foods. It's also important to store ingredients at the correct temperatures to prevent spoilage and bacterial growth. Make sure your staff is trained in food safety practices and that these practices are consistently followed.

Equipment Maintenance and Cleaning: Regular maintenance and cleaning of your coffee equipment are crucial for both safety and quality control. Coffee machines, grinders, and other equipment should be cleaned daily to prevent the buildup of coffee oils, milk residue, and bacteria. Additionally, equipment should be regularly inspected for signs of wear and tear, and any issues should be addressed promptly to prevent malfunctions or safety hazards.

Pest Control: Mobile food trucks can be particularly vulnerable to pests such as rodents and insects. To prevent infestations, ensure that your truck is thoroughly cleaned after each day of operation and that all food is stored in sealed containers. It's also important to conduct regular inspections of your truck and surrounding area to identify any potential pest entry points. If you do encounter a pest problem, address it immediately by working with a licensed pest control service.

Employee Health and Hygiene: Your staff plays a critical role in maintaining the health and safety of your coffee truck. Employees should be trained in proper hygiene practices, such as washing hands before handling food, wearing clean uniforms, and avoiding work when sick. It's also important to provide adequate facilities for handwashing, including soap, water, and disposable towels. Consider implementing a health policy that requires employees to report any illnesses that could affect food safety and to stay home if they are experiencing symptoms of contagious diseases.

Waste Disposal: Proper waste disposal is essential to maintain a clean and safe working environment. Your coffee truck should be equipped with appropriate waste containers for both regular trash and food waste. These containers should be emptied regularly, and waste should be disposed of in accordance with local regulations. Additionally, make sure to properly dispose of used oil, coffee grounds, and other waste materials that could attract pests or pose environmental hazards.

Compliance with Local Health Codes: Health codes vary by location, so it's important to familiarize yourself with the specific regulations in your area. These codes cover everything from food storage and preparation to waste disposal and pest control. Compliance with health codes is typically enforced through regular inspections by local health department officials. During an inspection, the official will assess your truck's cleanliness, equipment, food handling practices, and overall compliance with health regulations. It's important to be prepared for these inspections and to address any violations promptly to avoid penalties.

Health and safety regulations are designed to protect both your customers and your business. By adhering to these regulations, you can ensure that your coffee truck operates safely and that your customers have a positive and enjoyable experience.

Understanding Zoning Laws and Parking Restrictions

Zoning laws and parking restrictions play a significant role in determining where and when you can operate your coffee truck. These laws vary widely by location and are often one of the most challenging aspects of running a mobile food business. Understanding and complying with these regulations is essential to avoid fines and ensure that you're able to serve your customers without interruption.

Zoning Laws: Zoning laws dictate where food trucks can operate within a city or county. These laws are designed to manage traffic, noise, and the overall impact of mobile businesses on the community. Some areas may have designated zones where food trucks are allowed to operate, while others may restrict food trucks from operating near certain types of businesses, such as restaurants or schools. It's important to research the zoning laws in your area and obtain any necessary permits or approvals to operate in your desired locations.

Parking Restrictions: In addition to zoning laws, parking restrictions often apply to food trucks. These restrictions may include limits on how long you can park in a particular location, requirements for maintaining a certain distance from intersections or crosswalks, and rules about parking near fire hydrants or bus stops. Some cities also have designated parking spaces for food trucks, which may require a separate permit or fee. Be sure to familiarize yourself with the parking regulations in your area and plan your locations accordingly to avoid fines and ensure a smooth operation.

Operating in Public vs. Private Spaces: Food trucks can operate in both public and private spaces, but each comes with its own set of rules. Operating in public spaces, such as streets or parks, typically requires permits from the city or county. These permits may come with additional requirements, such as maintaining a certain distance from brick-and-mortar businesses or operating only during specific hours. Operating in private spaces, such as parking lots or events, may require permission from the property owner or event organizer. In some cases, you may also need to provide proof of insurance or sign a contract outlining the terms of your operation.

Event and Festival Regulations: Participating in events and festivals can be a lucrative opportunity for your coffee truck, but it often comes with additional regulations. Event organizers may have specific requirements for food vendors, such as obtaining a temporary permit, adhering to health and safety standards, and paying a vendor fee. It's also important to understand the logistics of operating at events, such as where you can park, how you'll access power and water, and what time you need to arrive and depart.

Navigating Multiple Jurisdictions: If you plan to operate your coffee truck in multiple cities or counties, you'll need to navigate the different regulations in each jurisdiction. This may involve obtaining multiple permits, understanding the zoning and parking laws in each area, and ensuring compliance with varying health and safety standards. It's a good idea to keep detailed records of your permits and licenses, as well as any communications with local authorities, to ensure you're always in compliance.

Understanding zoning laws and parking restrictions is essential to finding the best locations for your coffee truck and avoiding potential legal issues. By doing your research and staying informed, you can maximize your opportunities for success while minimizing the risk of fines and other penalties.

Liability Insurance and Risk Management

Running a coffee truck business comes with inherent risks, from accidents and injuries to equipment breakdowns and legal disputes. To protect your business, it's essential to have the right insurance coverage and to implement risk management strategies. This section will cover the types of insurance you need and how to manage the various risks associated with operating a mobile food business.

General Liability Insurance: General liability insurance is a must-have for any coffee truck business. This type of insurance covers bodily injury and property damage claims that may arise from your business operations. For example, if a customer slips and falls near your truck, or if you accidentally damage someone's property while operating, general liability insurance would cover the costs of legal fees, medical expenses, and any settlements or judgments. Having this coverage is crucial to protect your business from potentially devastating financial losses.

Commercial Auto Insurance: Since your coffee truck is a vehicle, you'll need commercial auto insurance to cover any accidents or damages that occur while driving. This insurance typically includes coverage for property damage, bodily injury, and collision damage. Depending on your policy, it may also cover theft, vandalism, and damage caused by natural disasters. It's important to choose a policy that provides adequate coverage for both your vehicle and any equipment or inventory inside the truck.

Property Insurance: Property insurance protects your coffee truck, equipment, and inventory from damage or loss due to fire, theft, vandalism, or other covered events. This coverage is essential for safeguarding your investment and ensuring that you can quickly recover and resume operations if something goes wrong. Be sure to review the specific terms of your policy, as some types of damage may require additional coverage or endorsements.

Workers' Compensation Insurance: If you have employees, workers' compensation insurance is typically required by law. This insurance covers medical expenses and lost wages for employees who are injured on the job. It also provides protection for your business by limiting your liability in the event of a workplace injury. Workers' compensation insurance is particularly important in a mobile food business, where employees may be exposed to risks such as burns, cuts, and lifting injuries.

Product Liability Insurance: Product liability insurance protects your business from claims related to the food and beverages you serve. For example, if a customer becomes ill after consuming one of your products, this insurance would cover the costs of legal defense, medical expenses, and any settlements or judgments. Product liability insurance is essential for any food service business, as it helps protect against the financial impact of foodborne illness claims and other product-related issues.

Risk Management Strategies: In addition to having the right insurance coverage, implementing risk management strategies can help reduce the likelihood of accidents, injuries, and other incidents. This includes regularly training your staff on safety procedures, conducting routine inspections of your truck and equipment, and maintaining detailed records of any incidents or near-misses. It's also important to develop a crisis management plan that outlines how you'll respond to emergencies, such as accidents, health violations, or natural disasters. Having a plan in place can help you respond quickly and effectively, minimizing the impact on your business.

By securing comprehensive insurance coverage and implementing proactive risk management strategies, you can protect your coffee truck business from unexpected events and ensure its long-term success.

"The road to success is paved with dedication and a great cup of coffee. Drive your dreams forward, one espresso at a time."

Chapter 5
Marketing and Building a Loyal Customer Base

Marketing and customer engagement are crucial to the success of your coffee truck business. To stand out in a competitive market and build a loyal following, you need to develop a compelling brand identity, effectively use digital marketing channels, and create memorable customer experiences. This chapter will guide you through these processes, helping you attract new customers and keep them coming back.

This Chapter focuses on the importance of marketing and customer engagement in building a successful coffee truck business. By developing a strong brand identity, leveraging digital marketing channels, creating memorable customer experiences, and measuring your marketing success, you can attract new customers and foster loyalty. Implementing these strategies will help you stand out in the market and build a thriving coffee truck business.

Crafting a Unique Brand Identity

Your brand identity is more than just a logo; it's the essence of your coffee truck's personality and the message you want to convey to your customers. A strong brand identity will make your business stand out and resonate with your target audience. Here's how to craft a compelling brand identity:

- **Establish Your Mission and Vision:** Start by defining the core purpose of your business (your mission) and what you hope to achieve in the long term (your vision). Your mission should articulate why your coffee truck exists and what it aims to provide. For instance, your mission might be to offer high-quality, sustainably sourced coffee with a focus on community engagement. Your vision could be to become a leading name in the local coffee scene or to expand to multiple locations.

- **Know Your Target Audience:** Understanding your target audience is key to developing a brand identity that appeals to them. Identify the demographics, interests, and preferences of your ideal customers. Are they busy professionals, college students, or coffee aficionados? Tailor your brand's voice, messaging, and visual elements to align with their expectations and preferences.

- **Design Your Visual Identity:** Your visual identity includes your logo, color palette, typography, and overall design style. These elements should be cohesive and reflect your brand's personality. For example, a modern coffee truck might use a sleek, minimalist logo with bold colors, while a more rustic brand might opt for a vintage design with earthy tones. Collaborate with a professional designer to create a visual identity that can be applied consistently across all platforms, including your truck, website, and marketing materials.

- **Develop a Brand Voice:** Your brand voice is how you communicate with your audience, both in written content and verbal interactions. It should reflect your brand's personality and resonate with your target market. Whether your tone is casual and friendly, professional and polished, or quirky and fun, consistency in your messaging will help build a recognizable and trustworthy brand.

Leveraging Digital Marketing Channels

Digital marketing is essential for reaching a broad audience and engaging with customers in today's tech-savvy world. Here's how to effectively utilize various digital marketing channels to promote your coffee truck business:

information about your coffee truck, such as your menu, location, hours of operation, and contact details. Incorporate engaging visuals and an easy-to-navigate layout to create a positive user experience. Additionally, consider adding a blog or news section to keep your customers updated on promotions, events, and new offerings.

Social media platforms are powerful tools for engaging with your audience and promoting your coffee truck.
Choose platforms that align with your target audience's preferences, such as Instagram for visual content, Facebook for community engagement, and Twitter for updates and interaction. Share high-quality photos of your coffee, behind-the-scenes content, customer testimonials, and special promotions. Engage with your followers by responding to comments and messages, and consider running contests or giveaways to boost engagement.

Email marketing allows you to stay in touch with your customers and keep them informed about your coffee truck. Build an email list by encouraging customers to subscribe through your website or social media. Send regular newsletters with updates on new menu items, special offers, and events. Personalize your emails to make them more engaging and relevant to your audience.

SEO helps improve your website's visibility on search engines like Google. Optimize your website with relevant keywords related to your coffee truck and its offerings. This includes using keywords in your website's content, meta descriptions, and image alt tags. Regularly updating your site with fresh content, such as blog posts or news updates, can also improve your search engine rankings.

Investing in Online Advertising: Online advertising can help you reach a larger audience and drive traffic to your website or social media profiles. Consider using pay-per-click (PPC) ads, social media ads, or display ads to promote your coffee truck. Target your ads based on factors like location, demographics, and interests to ensure they reach the right audience. Monitor the performance of your ads and adjust your strategy as needed to maximize your return on investment.

Creating Memorable Customer Experiences

Building a loyal customer base requires more than just good coffee; it's about creating positive and memorable experiences that keep people coming back. Here's how to enhance the customer experience at your coffee truck:

Offering Exceptional Service: Provide outstanding customer service by training your staff to be friendly, knowledgeable, and attentive. Encourage them to engage with customers, remember their preferences, and address any issues promptly. A positive interaction can turn a first-time customer into a regular.

Designing an Inviting Atmosphere: The ambiance of your coffee truck plays a significant role in customer satisfaction. Ensure that your truck is clean, well-organized, and visually appealing. Consider adding elements that enhance the customer experience, such as comfortable seating, pleasant music, or a unique theme that reflects your brand's personality.

Engaging with the Community: Build connections with your local community by participating in events, sponsoring local initiatives, or collaborating with other businesses. Engaging with the community helps create a positive image for your coffee truck and can attract new customers who value businesses that give back.

Encouraging Customer Feedback: Actively seek and listen to customer feedback to understand their needs and preferences. Provide easy ways for customers to share their opinions, such as comment cards, online surveys, or social media reviews. Use this feedback to make improvements and demonstrate that you value your customers' input.

Rewarding Loyalty: Implement a loyalty program to reward regular customers and encourage repeat business. This could include offering discounts, free items after a certain number of purchases, or exclusive promotions for loyal customers. A well-designed loyalty program can increase customer retention and drive more frequent visits.

Innovating and Adapting: Continuously look for ways to innovate and adapt your offerings to meet changing customer preferences and market trends. This could involve introducing new menu items, experimenting with seasonal specials, or incorporating feedback from your customers. Staying flexible and responsive to customer needs will help you maintain a competitive edge and keep your business fresh and exciting.

Measuring and Analyzing Marketing Success

To ensure that your marketing efforts are effective and to make informed decisions, it's important to measure and analyze your marketing performance. To track and evaluate your marketing success you have to learn and oblige by the following:

Setting Clear Goals: Define specific, measurable goals for your marketing efforts. These could include increasing website traffic, growing your social media following, boosting sales, or enhancing customer satisfaction. Having clear goals will help you focus your efforts and measure success more accurately.

Tracking Key Metrics: Use analytics tools to track key metrics related to your marketing activities. For your website, monitor metrics such as traffic, bounce rate, and conversion rates. For social media, track engagement metrics like likes, shares, comments, and follower growth. For email marketing, measure open rates, click-through rates, and conversion rates. Tracking these metrics will provide insights into what's working and what needs improvement.

Analyzing Campaign Performance: Regularly review the performance of your marketing campaigns to assess their effectiveness. Evaluate which channels and strategies are driving the best results and which ones may need adjustments. Use this data to refine your marketing approach and allocate resources more effectively.

Adjusting Your Strategy: Based on your analysis, make adjustments to your marketing strategy as needed. This could involve changing your messaging, trying new channels, or modifying your tactics to better align with your goals. Continuously optimizing your marketing efforts will help you stay competitive and achieve better results.

"When you start a business, you're not just selling a product; you're sharing a piece of your passion. Let your coffee truck be a testament to your dreams and your drive."

Chapter 6

Operational Efficiency and Scaling Your Coffee Truck Business.

Efficient operations are crucial for the success and growth of your coffee truck business. This chapter delves into the strategies and best practices for managing daily operations effectively, optimizing your workflow, and preparing for scaling your business. Whether you're looking to streamline your current operations or expand your coffee truck to new locations, understanding and implementing these principles will help you achieve long-term success.

Streamlining Daily Operations

Efficient daily operations are essential for running a smooth and profitable coffee truck business. Streamlining your processes helps reduce waste, increase productivity, and enhance customer satisfaction. Here's how to optimize your daily operations:

- **Establishing Standard Operating Procedures (SOPs):** Develop comprehensive SOPs for every aspect of your coffee truck operations, from opening and closing procedures to food preparation and customer service. SOPs ensure consistency, improve efficiency, and make it easier to train new staff. Document each procedure clearly, and review them regularly to make updates as needed.

- **Organizing Your Workflow:** Design your coffee truck's layout to maximize efficiency and minimize unnecessary movement. Place frequently used items, such as coffee beans and milk, within easy reach of your staff. Arrange your equipment and supplies in a logical order that follows the flow of your service process, from preparation to serving customers. A well-organized workspace reduces the time spent searching for items and helps prevent accidents.

- **Implementing Inventory Management:** Effective inventory management is key to reducing waste and ensuring that you have the right supplies on hand. Use an inventory tracking system to monitor stock levels, track usage, and manage reorders. Implement practices such as first-in, first-out (FIFO) to ensure that older stock is used before newer items. Regularly review your inventory data to identify trends and adjust your purchasing accordingly.

- **Training and Managing Staff:** Your staff plays a critical role in the daily operations of your coffee truck. Provide thorough training to ensure that they understand their responsibilities, the SOPs, and how to use the equipment effectively. Regularly assess their performance and provide feedback to help them improve. Foster a positive work environment by offering incentives, recognizing achievements, and addressing any issues promptly.

- **Maintaining Equipment:** Regular maintenance of your coffee truck's equipment is essential to prevent breakdowns and ensure optimal performance. Create a maintenance schedule that includes daily, weekly, and monthly tasks, such as cleaning, calibrating, and inspecting equipment. Address any issues immediately to avoid disruptions to your service.

Enhancing Customer Experience

Creating a positive and memorable customer experience is crucial for building loyalty and encouraging repeat business. Here's how to enhance the customer experience at your coffee truck:

Providing Excellent Customer Service: Train your staff to deliver exceptional customer service. This includes being friendly, attentive, and knowledgeable about your products. Encourage staff to engage with customers, remember their preferences, and address any concerns promptly. A positive interaction can significantly impact customer satisfaction and loyalty.

Offering a Consistent Product: Ensure that your coffee and other menu items are consistently high quality. Develop and follow standardized recipes and preparation techniques to maintain uniformity. Regularly review customer feedback and make adjustments as needed to meet their expectations.

Creating a Welcoming Atmosphere: The atmosphere of your coffee truck can enhance the overall customer experience. Ensure that your truck is clean, visually appealing, and comfortable. Consider adding elements that make the experience enjoyable, such as a unique design theme, ambient music, or friendly staff interactions.

Implementing Customer Feedback Mechanisms: Encourage customers to provide feedback on their experience. This can be done through comment cards, online surveys, or social media reviews. Use this feedback to make improvements and address any issues. Showing that you value and act on customer input can build trust and loyalty.

Scaling Your Coffee Truck Business

Once your coffee truck business is running smoothly, you may consider scaling to expand your reach and increase your revenue. Scaling involves more than just adding more trucks; it requires strategic planning and effective management. Here's how to prepare for and manage growth:

Outline a clear growth strategy that defines your expansion goals and objectives. Decide whether you want to open additional trucks, expand to new locations, or both. Assess your market potential and identify areas where there is demand for your coffee. Develop a detailed plan that includes timelines, budgets, and key milestones.

Expanding your coffee truck business often requires additional capital. Explore different financing options, such as loans, investors, or crowdfunding. Prepare a detailed business plan and financial projections to present to potential investors or lenders. Ensure that you have a clear understanding of the costs involved in scaling and how you will manage the financial aspects of the expansion.

As you add more trucks, maintaining consistency and quality across locations becomes crucial. Develop standardized procedures and training programs for new staff. Implement systems for inventory management, equipment maintenance, and customer service that can be replicated across all trucks. Regularly review operations to ensure that each truck adheres to your brand standards.

Expanding your coffee truck business requires efficient management of logistics and supply chains. Coordinate deliveries and inventory management to ensure that each truck receives the necessary supplies in a timely manner. Consider working with reliable suppliers and logistics partners to streamline the process and reduce disruptions.

As you scale, it's important to monitor and analyze the performance of each truck and location. Use key performance indicators (KPIs) to track metrics such as sales, customer satisfaction, and operational efficiency. Regularly review this data to identify areas for improvement and make informed decisions about your expansion strategy.

A successful expansion requires a strong and dedicated team. Hire and train staff who are aligned with your brand values and are capable of managing multiple locations. Foster a positive work culture and provide opportunities for career growth and development. A motivated and skilled team will contribute to the success of your expanded operations.

Managing Challenges During Growth

Scaling your coffee truck business presents unique challenges that need to be managed effectively. Here are common challenges and strategies for overcoming them:

Maintaining Quality Control: As you expand, maintaining the same level of quality across all locations can be challenging. Implement strict quality control measures and regular audits to ensure consistency. Provide ongoing training and support to your staff to uphold your brand's standards.

Managing Increased Complexity: Operating multiple trucks introduces additional complexity in logistics, staffing, and operations. Develop robust systems and processes to handle this complexity efficiently. Use technology, such as management software and communication tools, to streamline operations and keep track of various aspects of your business.

Adapting to Market Changes: The market environment may change as you expand, requiring you to adapt your strategies. Stay informed about industry trends, customer preferences, and competitive dynamics. Be flexible and willing to adjust your approach based on market conditions and feedback.

Balancing Growth and Cash Flow: Rapid growth can strain your cash flow and financial resources. Monitor your financials closely and manage your cash flow to ensure that you have the resources needed for expansion. Plan for contingencies and avoid overextending yourself financially.

Conclusively, this chapter provides a comprehensive guide to operational efficiency and scaling your coffee truck business. By streamlining daily operations, enhancing the customer experience, planning for growth, and managing challenges, you can build a successful and scalable coffee truck business. Implementing these strategies will help you achieve long-term success and reach your expansion goals.

"Every great business begins with a single idea and a lot of hard work. Your coffee truck is the beginning of something extraordinary."

CONCLUSION

Embarking on the journey of starting a coffee truck business is both an exciting and challenging venture. By now, you've walked through the essential steps, from conceptualizing your coffee truck idea to understanding the financial intricacies, acquiring necessary permits, and crafting a unique brand that resonates with your target audience. The information laid out in this book is designed to equip you with the foundational knowledge and practical tools to transform your dream into a reality.

The Journey from Vision to Execution

Starting a coffee truck business begins with a vision—an idea of the perfect cup of coffee, the ideal customer experience, and the freedom of operating your own mobile business. Turning this vision into a successful reality requires careful planning, attention to detail, and a willingness to adapt. From the initial stages of market research to finding the right vehicle, sourcing high-quality ingredients, and perfecting your menu, every step contributes to the bigger picture of your business's success.

Building a Strong Foundation

Your coffee truck is more than just a vehicle; it's a business on wheels that requires a solid foundation. This includes creating a business plan that outlines your objectives, financial projections, marketing strategies, and operational procedures. A well-thought-out plan not only guides your day-to-day activities but also serves as a crucial tool when seeking financing or partnerships.

Securing permits, licenses, and ensuring compliance with local health regulations are non-negotiable steps in establishing a legitimate and trustworthy business. This foundation of legality and professionalism will earn the trust of your customers and set the stage for long-term success.

Crafting Your Unique Brand

In the competitive world of mobile coffee businesses, your brand is what sets you apart. Your brand encompasses your logo, truck design, menu, and customer service philosophy. It's the story you tell and the experience you offer. Consistency in branding helps build customer loyalty and makes your coffee truck a memorable destination rather than just a quick stop for coffee.

Whether you choose to focus on specialty coffees, organic ingredients, or a particular theme, your brand should reflect your passion and values. This authenticity will resonate with your customers, turning first-time visitors into regular patrons.

Financial Management and Growth

Understanding the financial aspects of running a coffee truck is crucial for sustainability and growth. From managing startup costs to tracking daily sales, every financial decision impacts your bottom line. Setting up efficient accounting practices and regularly reviewing your financial statements will help you stay on top of your business's financial health.

As your business grows, consider expanding your offerings, exploring new locations, or even adding additional trucks to your fleet. Each of these growth opportunities comes with its own set of challenges, but with the knowledge you've gained, you'll be well-prepared to navigate them successfully.

Adapting to Challenges

The coffee truck business, like any other, comes with its unique set of challenges. Whether it's fluctuating weather conditions, competition, or changes in consumer preferences, your ability to adapt will be key to your long-term success. Flexibility in your operations, willingness to experiment with new ideas, and staying attuned to your customers' needs will help you overcome obstacles and seize new opportunities.

The Road Ahead

As you prepare to launch your coffee truck, remember that this is just the beginning. The road ahead will be filled with learning experiences, both rewarding and challenging. The skills you've developed in planning, marketing, financial management, and customer service will serve you well as you navigate the ups and downs of the business.

Success in the coffee truck industry doesn't happen overnight. It's the result of persistent effort, continuous learning, and a passion for what you do. By staying committed to your vision and being open to growth and innovation, you can build a thriving coffee truck business that brings joy to your customers and fulfillment to you as an entrepreneur.

Starting a coffee truck business is an adventure that combines creativity, business acumen, and a love for coffee. This book has provided you with a comprehensive guide to get started, but the real learning happens out on the road, interacting with customers, and refining your craft.

Believe in your vision, stay resilient, and enjoy the journey. With dedication, hard work, and a passion for delivering great coffee, your coffee truck business can become a beloved staple in your community and beyond. Here's to your success on this exciting entrepreneurial path!

www.ingramcontent.com/pod-product-compliance
Lightning Source LLC
Chambersburg PA
CBHW081019240526
45471CB00017B/3427